THE DEVIL IN THE DETAILS,

Tensions between the Bankruptcy Code & Environmental Law Claims

By: Dale D. McGinnis

INTRODUCTION

For Bankruptcies, whether the EPA, SEC, or DOJ comes knocking on your door, (or) whether you are on the other side of the regulator's table; (or) whether you are turning corners for the Government; everyone is left to the will of a Bear-of-a-statute ("CERCLA") in the Woods with a framework and 'fresh-start' ("Bankruptcy Code"). Whether the environment- contaminated, abandoned, and so forth- is treated as a claim is a question where tensions exist between CERCLA & the Bankruptcy Code (and) where the Devil is in the Details.

Last year, Fossil Fuel companies were the talk all around Ch. 11 town. *The New York Times* highlighted what some environmentalist's and scholar's believed to be the fall of 'King Coal'[1] by 'market forces'[2]. *The New York Times* also highlighted other international religion institutions

---

[1] James B. Stewart, King Coal, "Deposed by the Market", *The New York Times*, Aug. 6, 2015 (http://www.nytimes.com/2015/08/07/business/energy-environment/coal-industry-wobbles-as-market-forces-slug-away.html?_r=0).
- Collapsing prices and heavy debt loads are driving industry into bankruptcy
- Market forces accomplish what EL's and SA's could not do in decades

[2] *See* Id.

that seemed to jump on the bandwagon[3]. Further, the *New York Times* highlighted specifically an anticipated flip in this commodities market[4].

With the anticipation of Bankruptcy; anticipation of EL claims; and an interest to explore all alternatives to save the Estate; how can a Fossil Fuel (Company (or) an individual (or) another entity owning interest therein) survive?

To answer this broad question: we have to understand 1) the Lions, Tigers, & Bears[5], that is, the authority and reasoning behind Administrative agency laws, such as CERCLA & RCRA; 2) the Woods[6], that is, the bankruptcy code and how it applies to Environmental issues, such as impact reports or cleanups as dischargeable claims; and finally; 3) the tensions between the two[7],

---

[3] Kate Column, "Churches Go Green by Shedding Fossil Fuel Holdings", *The New York Times*, Oct. 15, 2014 (http://www.nytimes.com/2014/10/16/business/international/churches-go-green-by-shedding-holdings-of-carbon-emitters.html).
- Church of Sweden after conference removes fossil fuel companies from Church's financial portfolio
- Began with universities, now religious institutions including but not limited to: Presbyterian Church of New Zealand (considering) and Anglican Diocese of Perth (divesting interest in fossil fuels)
    - Not going to bankrupt fossil fuels, but "has the effect of getting people to stop and think"

[4] Clifford Krauss & Ian Austen, "If it Owns a Well or a Mine, It's Probably in Trouble", *The New York Times*, Dec. 8, 2015 (http://www.nytimes.com/2015/12/09/business/anglo-american-to-cut-85000-jobs-amid-commodity-slump.html).
- World of commodities upside down
- Tight supply and strong demand -> tepid demand and oversupply; and
- Over capacity for commodity production
    - Commodity = a raw material or primary agricultural product that can be bought and sold, such as copper or coffee
    - Commodity production (also known as "petty commodity") = simple exchange of commodities, where independent producers trade their own products

[5] *See* Infra at 3.
[6] *See* Infra at 7.
[7] *See* Infra at 13.

that is, the interplay between these beasts of statute in the furtherance of the Administrative policy and goal, bankruptcy code's policy and rules, and the corporation's fiduciary duty to its shareholders or vise versa.

First, we shall discuss a brief history of CERCLA[8]. Second, we shall discuss overview of the relevant provisions of the Bankruptcy Code[9]. Third, we shall discuss interplay and tension between EL & BC[10].

I. LIONS, TIGERS, & CERCLA

The Comprehensive Environmental Response, Compensation, and Liability Act of 1980 ("CERCLA") was passed by Congress as a result of waste being dumped out on the land, in the rivers, and in the open.[11] Congress' response(s), creating the Superfund in 1980 and the Environmental Protection Agency, because of the growing concern over health (and) the environmental risks posed by these waste site(s).[12]

---

[8] *See* infra at 3.
[9] *See* infra at 7.
[10] *See* infra at 13.
[11] Benivia, LLC, "CERCLA- The Comprehensive Environmental Response, Compensation, and Liability Act Overview", Environmental Health & Safety Online ("EHSO"), updated Mar. 30, 2016 (http://www.ehso.com/superfund.php).
- chemists, engineers and environmental professionals
- believe that factual, verifiable and easy-to-understand information needs to be provided to the public to help people make better decisions about the products and services they buy and their family's health
- non-profit
- Contact info: EPA, State agencies (OSHA & DOT)
- Regulators: government regs and sites
- Data: EPA and seminars and conferences

[12] *See* Id. at Purpose and Organization

Not just any statute, CERCLA uses the Comprehensive Environmental Response, Compensation, and liability Information System ("CERCLIS") for site and non-site specific Superfund data[13]. Administrative agencies utilize this information from this database & a fund of 1.6 Billion out of the Nation's budget, through an excise tax, to pay for cleanup activities at abandoned waste sites.[14]

Or, CERLCA may require Potential Responsible Parties ("PRP's") to conduct a cleanup over these waste sites (or) pay someone else to do it- like the Superfund[15]. Like an efficient beast, CERCLA provides and establishes the prohibitions and requirements for closed and abandoned hazardous waste sites (and) which and when the party responsible and liable, may use the trust fund to provide for the cleanup where no responsible party comes forward or can be pointed out[16].

To identify the type of cleanup necessary, CERCLA classifies response actions into two categories: short-term (or) long-term removals removals where actions may be taken to address release or threatened releases requiring prompt responses to permanently and significantly reduce the dangers associated with releases or threats of releases of hazardous substances that are serious, but not immediately life threatening[17]. Additionally, cleanups by the superfund can only be conduct on sites listed on the EPA's National Priorities list ("NPL")[18].

To response to cleanups, the Enabled revision of National Contingency Plan ("NCP") provides guidelines and procedures needed to respond to releases and threated releases of

---

[13] *See* Id. at Introduction
[14] *See* Id. at Response Efforts and National Contingency Plan
[15] *See* Id. at supra Requires
[16] *See* Id. at supra Provides and Establishes
[17] *See* Id. at supra Enabled revision of National Contingency Plan
[18] *See* Id.

hazardous substances, pollutants, or contaminants[19]. It describing the steps for PRP's[20]. There, the NCP establishes criteria, methods, and procedures for the PRP's[21]. The EPA uses the NCP to determine priority releases for long-term evaluation and response, where the national goal is to select remedies that protect human health and the environment- minimizing untreated waste and providing protection over time[22]. There, the NCP categories removal actions in three ways: emergency removal, time-critical, and non-time-critical removal actions, where the categories are based on the type of situation, urgency of the threat of release, and subsequent time frame in which action must be initiated[23].

NCP's remedial actions includes: discovery, selection, study, design, and construction of longer-term actions aimed at a permanent remedy[24]. The superfund's remedial process includes: preliminary assessment, site inspection, hazard ranking system, national priorities list, remedial investigation, feasibility study, record of decision, remedial design, and remedial action.[25]. The EPA refers to the National Priorities List before and after site completion, for reference and deletion upon cleanup[26].

Under CERCLA and implemented by the NCP, the Natural Resource Damage Assessment allows federal or state officials or Indian tribes appointed as trustees for the natural resources can assess damages[27].

---

[19] *See* Id. at supra Amended by Superfund Amendments and Reauthorization Act ("SARA")
[20] *See* Id. at supra Categories of Removal Actions
[21] *See* Id. at supra Requirements
[22] *See* id.
[23] *See* Id. at supra Categories of Removal Actions
[24] *See* Id. at supra Remedial Actions
[25] *See* Id. at supra Superfund Remedial Process
[26] *See* Id. at Site Completion and Deletion from the NPL
[27] *See* Id. at Natural Resource Damage Assessment

Further, the EPA will not take enforcement action against landowners and transferee's who acquire contaminated property from a federal agency, unless they contribute or cause a new contamination[28]. Pending legislation in senate and the house, there is the information on the internet[29]. CERCLA requires the PRP's to release a report to the NRC in event of a release which exceed Reported Qualities ("RQ's")[30].

These reports may trigger a response by the EPA or a state emergency response authority[31]. Guided by the NCP, the EPA or state emergency response authorizes or the PRP's remove the hazardous substances[32]. The EPA specifically only reports to the 1,300 sites posted on the NPL and gives PRP's opportunity (and) encourages community involvement in the process[33].

The Superfund Amendment AND Reauthorization Act of 1986 ("SARA") expanded the federal government's response authority and clarified that federal facilities are subject to same requirements as private industries[34]. Additionally, Congress has continued to extend this authority. Authority extended by congress by four-year extension in 1990[35]

SARA gives the NCP the authority for the following response actions: program to report the spills of hazardous substances, emergency response program to cleanup releases of hazardous substances, and a remedial program for the permanent cleanup of releases from closed or abandoned hazardous waste disposal sites[36].

---

[28] *See* Id. at Policy Towards Landowners and Transferees of Federal Facilities
[29] *See* Id at Superfund Reform and Reauthorization
[30] *See* Id.
[31] *See* Id. at supra Hazardous Substance Release Reporting Regulations
[32] *See* Id.
[33] *See* Id at supra Hazardous Substance Responses
[34] *See* Id. at supra National Oil and Hazardous Substances Pollution Contingency Plan ("NCP")
[35] *See* Id. at supra Response Actions
[36] *See* Id. at supra Response Actions

The Community Environmental Response Facilitation Act of 1992 ("CERFA"), amended CERCLA to expedite the sale of excess property, allowing uncontaminated property to be sold before cleanup of the whole facility is completed, where the federal government most identify the parts of the real property where no hazardous substance has been stored, released, or disposed of[37]. There, CERCLA requires only the extent of remedial action necessary to protect human health and the environment on property where hazardous substances were[38]. In fact, the Hall Amendment, allows the DOE to lease property if it is temporarily not needed or excess once the Secretary consults with the Administrator of the Environmental Protection Agency to determine whether the environmental conditions of the property are consistent with safety and the protection of public health and the environment[39].

An additional statute, the Resource Conservation and Recovery Act, was enacted by Congress to reduce the generation of waste and regulate the proper disposal, treatment, and storage of waste[40].

II. The Woods: A Framework & a 'Fresh-Start', but what EL claim?

The Bankruptcy Code stands as a framework for resolving a debtor's pre-bankruptcy liabilities affording the debtor a "fresh start"[41]. The "fresh start" discharges the debtor of liability for actual and contingent claim(s) arising prepetition, that is, before the bankruptcy petition was filed[42].

---

[37] *See* Id.
[38] *See* Id. at Community Environmental Response Facilitation Act of 1992 ("CERFA")
[39] *See* Id. at Hall Amendment
[40] *See* Id.
[41] Environmental Aspects of Real Estate and Commercial Transactions (James B. Witkin ed., 4th ed. 2011).
[42] *See* Id.

The framework provides for a liquidation or reorganization of the debtor's assets and allocation of assets among all the creditors[43]. With respect to Environmental liabilities, whether those liabilities constitute a claim(s) and whether those liabilities arose prepetition are imperative questions[44]. If so, the Creditor's claims by extension of the debtor will be subject to discharge or payment claims[45].

A liability on a claim by the Creditor's or the debtor is debt by definition[46]. Claims, however, by definition are rights to payment (or) right to an equitable remedy for breach of performance if it gives rise to a payment, whether or not any of those rights are reduced to judgment(s) of any kind[47]. Unless a future event triggers the debtor's legal duty to pay, the parties must have actually or presumably contemplated this future event during the time the relationship was established[48].

The debtor's legal obligation is trigged by any required clean up of hazardous substances, as defined by the Bankruptcy code and required by other nonbankruptcy law[49]. If the contamination of hazardous substance occurred prepetition, it is presumed a general unsecured claim[50]. Following, the EPA's ability to recover their cost for cleanup depends on whether the they are considered a creditor (or) whether payment rights will be discharged[51].

---

[43] *See* Id.
[44] *See* Id.
[45] *See* Id.
[46] *See* Id.
[47] *See* Id.
[48] *See* Id.
[49] *See* Id.
[50] *See* Id.
[51] *See* Id.

The courts look towards the Bankruptcy Code's expresses a strong and clear congressional intent that upon Confirmation a debtor be discharged form all claims "actual and contingent"[52]. Within that broad concept of a 'claim', arise the following questions: A claim arises when cleanup costs are incurred[53]; a Claim Arises at the Time Hazardous Substances Are Released[54]; Unincurred Costs Are Dischargeable in Bankruptcy[55]; and EPA May Recover Future Response Costs[56].

A. What Site(s)?: United States v. Union Scrap Iron[57]

Who is the PRP? Prepetition release of hazardous substances prior to bankruptcy reorganization does not give rise to CERCLA claims. These claims would be dischargable upon confirmation, but the EPA does not know who the PRP's are.

Here: EPA attempted to collect 1.2million from 20 defendants. Because Taracorp's reorganization plan was confirmed in July 1985, and it did not file claims with respect to those sites (the order discharged the claims)[58]. However, Taraciro's disclosure statement and plan of reorganization did not mention potential environmental liabilities[59]. And, EPA did not file a prospective claim with the bankruptcy court, any liability for hazardous substance cleanup cost was discharged when the court confirmed Taracorp's reorganization plan[60].

EPA argued the bankruptcy proceeding only involved two facilities, and not the activities

---

[52] See Id.
[53] See Id.
[54] See Id.
[55] See Id.
[56] See Id.
[57] United States v. Union Scrap Iron & Metal, 123 B.R. 831 (D. Minnesota 1990).
[58] See Id.
[59] See Id.
[60] See Id.

on the Union Scrape site[61]. Further arguing under CERCLA, the right is not triggered until costs incur "mere release" of a hazardous substance was insufficient. Liabilities arose at the time EPA incurred those costs[62]. Taracorp argued EPA could presume Taracorp was involvement in the union Scrap site was apart of the original negotiation[63]. However, the court disagreed disregarding this argument as inconceivable enforcement action[64].

B. Right to Payment (or) Conduct, special status: In re Jensen[65]

A Claim arose for purposes of bankruptcy "at the time of actual or threatened release of the hazardous waste or based upon the debtor's conduct," even if cleanup costs were incurred postpetition. Three theories as to when a bankruptcy claim arises: 1) right to payment, 2) upon established relationship between debtor and creditor[66].

Here, DHS argued the first theory. The court agreed, because § 101(4), "requires a right to payment before a claim is recognized in bankruptcy, and the right to payment under federal or state law did not arise until cleanup costs are incurred, no claim existed for bankruptcy purposes until those cleanup costs are incurred"[67].

The appellate panel found the third theory satisfies the BC's legislative intent[68]. Relying on *In re Jogn-Manville Corp.*[69], and *In re A.H. Robins Co.*[70] "right to payment" arose at the time when the acts giving rise to the alleged liability occurred[71]. The Bankruptcy appellate panel

---

[61] See Id.
[62] See Id.
[63] See Id.
[64] See Id.
[65] In re Jensen, 23 ELR 20991.
[66] See Id.
[67] See Id.
[68] See Id.
[69] In Re Johns-Manville Corp., 33 B.R. 254 (Bankr. S.D.N.Y. 1983)
[70] In Re A.h. Robins Company, Incorporated, Debtor, 880 F.2d 709 (4th Cir. 1989)
[71] *See* Id. at FN Supra 68.

rejected this theory because it would trigger recognition of the bankruptcy claim "contravenes the overriding goal of the Bankruptcy Code to provide a 'fresh start' fro the debtor"[72]. Pointing to the definition of a "claim" in BC § 101(4) includes contingent and matured right to payment[73].

However, Jensen[74], held otherwise[75]. The claims arose based on the debtor's prepetition conduct and therefore was discharged in bankruptcy[76]. No cause of action arose until there was a release or a threatened release of a hazardous substance[77]. DHS and the bankruptcy court believed that the public policies supporting environmental cleanup afforded environmental claims a special status, where Jensen relied on the Ninth Circuit's precedent stating, "sounded a strong policy against according preference to particular claims" within a specifically enumerated class- absent a clear directive[78].

Therefore, since claims in bankruptcy arose based on the debtor's conduct, DHS' claim arose prepetition and was discharged by the debtor's bankruptcy[79].

C. To Remedy any Restricts: **In re Chateaugay Corp.**[80]

As long as "response costs" relate to a prepetition release or threatened release of hazardous substances, they can be properly characterized as prepetition claims and dischargeable in bankruptcy[81]. EPA argued that CERCLA's would be better off if they could assert reimbursement claims for response costs instead arguing for a narrower reading of CERCLA

---

[72] *See* Id.
[73] *See* Id.
[74] *See* Id.
[75] *See* Id.
[76] *See* Id.
[77] *See* Id.
[78] *See* Id.
[79] *See* Id.
[80] In re In re Chateaugay Corp., 21 ELR 21466.
[81] *See* Id.

further Congress' objectives[82]. However, the court is bound to construe the Bankruptcy Code "fairly" and avoid a restrictive reading[83]. Congress' role is remedying any restriction in the BC on Environmental cleanup efforts[84].

D. In or Out: In re National Gyposum Co.

Entitled to collect a sum certain for future response costs and natural resources damages costs from the debtor[85]. Here: 20 sites, 7 CERCLA sites filed[86]. Upon filing bankruptcy contacted EPA to announce their potential CERCLA liability[87]. Expressly reserved right to assert due to prepetition conduct with respect to 13 unlisted sites[88].

The following issues, therefore, with respect to that conduct is: listed sites = claim[89]; unlisted sites = claim[90]; response costs = administrative expense priority[91]; debtors = jointly and severally liable[92]; and US argued future response costs and future natural resources damages costs at listed site were not dischargable claims, but the response costs incurred afterward were entitled to administrative priority [93]. Additionally the debtors were jointly and severally liable[94].

Debtors argued opposite: these costs and damages for the listed sites were prepetition claims subject to discharge, their environmental liabilities arising from conduct were claims, the response costs incurred afterwards should be fixed at an amount, and the proof of claim should

---

[82] *See* Id.
[83] *See* Id.
[84] *See* Id.
[85] In Re National Gypsum Co., (257 BR 184 – BANKR. COURT, ND TEXAS, 2000).
[86] *See* Id.
[87] *See* Id.
[88] *See* Id.
[89] *See* Id.
[90] *See* Id.
[91] *See* Id.
[92] *See* Id.
[93] *See* Id.
[94] *See* Id.

be fixed as well to an amount reflecting the debtors' equitable share of liability[95]. The court, relying on *Union Scrap*[96], holding since BC encompassed the term claim all contingent, unliquidated, and unmatured right to payment[97].

An expansive reading of a "claim" leaves a prepetition release, unknown to anyone[98]. *National Gypsum*[99] set forth the following factors to determine whether costs were within the parties' fair contemplation: knowledge; NPL listing; Notice; Investigation or cleanup activities or incurred response costs[100]. With respect to the US: knowledge; NPL listing Commencement; and Conduct = fairly contemplated by the parties[101].

III. The Woods [102]

When entering the Woods, the following B.C. concepts as applied to EL claims make seeing the trees through the forest a difficult task.

A. **Administrative priority status; necessary to preserve the Estate**[103]

The Bankruptcy Court looks at where abandonment of contaminated property is burdensome to the estate or is of inconsequential value and benefit to the estate- trustee may abandon[104]. The Supreme Court- sees it differently- holding no one in possession of a site may

---

[95] *See* Id.
[96] *See* Id.
[97] *See* Id.
[98] *See* Id.
[99] *See* Id.
[100] *See* Id.
[101] *See* Id.
[102] Christine L. Childers & Keri L. Holleb Hotaling, "Treatment of Environmental Obligations in Bankruptcy", Environmental Law in Illinois Corporate and Real Estate Transactions, 14th edition, Ch. 10, IICLE Press (http://www.iicle.com/environmental-law-in-illinois-corporate-and-real-estate-transactions-2014-edition).
[103] *See* Id. at 343.
[104] *See* Id. at 344

avoid compliance with the environmental laws[105]. The statutory obligations, therefore, will survive bankruptcy[106].

The exceptions are narrow[107]. Where PRP's must formulate conditions to adequately protect public' health and safety[108]. Where abandonment would not create an imminent harm or danger to the public. SC: the BC does not authorize the abandonment of burdensome property in contravention of state environmental laws when cleanup costs would exceed the estate's equity[109].

Therefore, an estate with unencumbered assets will likely be required to follow a stricter compliance with the EL before abandonment will be permitted[110]. The abandon property reverts to the debtor or other person or entity, and is no longer property of the estate[111]. And, the environmental response costs incurred after that date will not have administrative priority status because such are not necessary to preserve the property of the estate[112].

B. An apparent struggle: imminent environmental threats & the police power exception[113]

Here, there is an apparent struggle to balance the competing public policy interests: Full benefits of the stay relief, and Protecting the environment and human health and safety, by minimizing obstacles to prompt abatement of imminent environmental threats[114]. Automatic stay

---

[105] *See* Id.
[106] *See* Id.
[107] *See* Id.
[108] *See* Id.
[109] *See* Id.
[110] *See* Id.
[111] *See* Id.
[112] *See* Id.
[113] *See* Id. 345
[114] *See* Id.

generally operates as a stay of any actions. It does not against a governmental body -> policy powers, other than monetary judgment[115].

Historically, the right to payment is equivalent to monetary judgment and thus exempt from police power exception[116]. The majority: money judgment is defined narrowly and have refused to extend protection[117]. And, the trend: consists with debtor's obligation manage and operate estate property in compliance with environmental and state laws[118].

C. Accountability[119]

RCRA and some state laws require in many industries to pledge and maintain sufficient financial resources to address contingent environmental liabilities, such as the financial assurances necessary to close or abandon a facility in an environmentally responsible fashion[120]

However, tensions rise when the governmental asserts the police power exception to the stay, compelling the debtor to satisfy RCRA (or) risk exposure and revocation of permits critical to operate[121]. In a pinch, the debtor can use cash collateral for obligations in exchange for a layer of protection for its securities[122]. For the individual (or) entity, however, commencement tor continuation of actions against debtor or estate is stayed, until modification[123]. The PRP groups and members are left to file and pursue proof of claim in the bankruptcy case[124].

D. Shed and Reduce[125]

---

[115] *See* Id.
[116] *See* Id.
[117] *See* Id.
[118] *See* Id.
[119] *See* Id. at 345
[120] *See* Id.
[121] *See* Id.
[122] *See* Id.
[123] *See* Id.
[124] *See* Id.
[125] *See* Id. at 345

Whether the debtor can effectively shed or significantly reduce oppressive environmental obligations through bankruptcy, in confirmation of a Chapter 11 debtor's plan of reorganization, generally discharges the debtor only from claims with respect arose before the confirmation date, by claim holders with adequate notice, and had the opportunity to participate in the case[126]. For, Chapter 7 only to claims with respect arose prepetition[127].

Whether the environmental liability at issue is a "claim" under the BC, stems from the distinction between a creditor's right to recover cleanup costs, that is, its right to the payment of money, and its right to injunctive relief compelling the debtor to abate and clean up pollution[128].

Unless an injunction can be converted to a money judgment, it is not a "right to payment" within the statutory definition of "claim" under existing case law[129]. Whether the claim arose before or after plan confirmation (and) whether the creditor holding the claim had sufficient notice of the case and the debtor's liability to participate meaningfully in the bankruptcy proceedings, arise postbankrupcty[130]. These challenges, put the debtor's relationship to the site or the creditor in question, that is, was not, or could not have been, known before the bankruptcy (or) a combination of any of these grounds[131].

E. The Dual Objectives[132]

A "claim" is defined broadly in the Code to include: 1) right to payment, whether or not such right is reduced to judgment; or 2) right to an equitable remedy for breach of performance if

---

[126] *See* Id.
[127] *See* Id.
[128] *See* Id.
[129] *See* Id.
[130] *See* Id.
[131] *See* Id.
[132] *See* Id. at 346

such breach gives rise to a right to payment, whether or not such right to an equitable remedy is reduced to judgment[133].

Generally, courts hold debtor's obligation s is not a claim within the meaning of the BC, and therefore not dischargeable[134]. The supreme Court held the debtor's obligation to perform cleanup work at a contaminated site pursuant to a prepetition order was dischargable[135]. The court relied on liability had been reduced to a demand for money and limited dischrageability only to hose parts of the cleanup order that involved the collection of money[136].

The 2nd Circuit held that injunctive remedies may be discharable if the government has the option to perform the remediation and recover costs from the debtor, "cleanup order that accomplishes the dual objectives of removing accumulated wastes and stopping ameliorating ongoing pollution emanating from such wastes is not a dischargeable claim"[137].

On the other hand, a cleanup order that imposes obligations distinct from the obligations to stop ongoing pollution is a "claim if the agency had the option to do the cleanup work and sue the corporation for response costs"[138].

However, even when seeking these costs postpetition, CERCLA gives the federal government the option to conduct site investigations and remediation and sue responsible parties for reimbursement for response costs like comparable state statutes, although those state statutes- under Chateaugay I guidance- do not give the government the option to accept payment from a

---

[133] *See* Id. (liquidated, unliquidated, fixed, contingent, matured, unmatured, disputed, undisputed, legal, equitable, secured, or unsecured)
[134] *See* Id.
[135] *See* Id.
[136] *See* Id.
[137] *See* Id.
[138] *See* Id. (predicted that most injunctions would "fall on the non-claim' side of the line" because most cleanup orders include obligations to remove or remediate contaminated soil or other sources from which pollution continues to emanate)

liable party in lieu of addressing ongoing pollution leaching, migrating, or otherwise emanating from accumulated wastes at a site[139].

F. To Identify & To Disclose [140]

Debtor is bound by certain due process requirements (compliance minimizes risk prepetition obligations survive after bankruptcy): 1) to identify in its schedules all creditors, 2) to notify all creditors and parties-in-interest of the filing of the case, 3) and the date by which proof of claim must be filled (the "bar date")[141].

If fail, a holder of a claim may not be bound by the debtor's discharge[142]. Otherwise, the claimant must file a proof of claim by the bar date to preserve its claim and the right to participate in bankruptcy distributions[143]. This means, a reasonable search for contingent or unmatured claims so that ascertainable creditors can receive actual notice of the date[144].

A creditor is known or unknown is determined by whether, at the time the petition's filing, the creditor's identify is either known or ascertainable by the debtor, reasonably ascertainable if that creditor can be identified through reasonably diligent efforts[145]. Unknown creditors have claims that are either conjectural or will arise in the future or that do not, in the due course of business, come to the debtor's knowledge[146]. Therefore, notice by publication is sufficient to known creditors[147].

---

[139] *See* Id.
[140] *See* Id. at 348
[141] *See* Id.
[142] *See* Id.
[143] *See* Id.
[144] *See* Id.
[145] *See* Id.
[146] *See* Id.
[147] *See* Id. (because the existence and scope of a debtor's environmental liability at a site may not be discoverable or fully known for several years after the release of contaminants into the environment)

G. An Uncertain Estimation[148]

The allowabillity in bankruptcy of claims against the debtor is determined by the bankruptcy court using federal bankruptcy laws. In order to avoid undue delay in the administration of the case and the cost of litigation, these claims that could give rise to questions about the feasibility of the reorganization plan are determined in estimation hearings[149]. Therefore, the Courts have a great deal of discretion in selecting the procedures for a claim estimation proceeding[150]. However, because of uncertainty with the debtor's liability[151]. And, in the absence of proving the likelihood of success on the merits, claims may be estimated at zero.

H. Co-Liability[152]

In parts, §502(e)(1)(B) states, contingent claims of parties co-liable with the debtor for reimbursement or contribution are disallowed[153]. The purpose to avoid duplicate claims against the debtor for the same indebtedness[154]. If the bankruptcy petition was filed before PRP liability is determine or costs have incurred, the claim for contribution or reimbursement was contingent[155].

Therefore, because a PRP seeking contribution will be reluctant to offer evidence of its own exposure of liability for cleanup costs where its liability to the government has not been

---

[148] *See* Id. at 349.
[149] *See* Id. (the amount of a claim should be estimated in accordance with the statute or common law from which it arises)
[150] *See* Id.
[151] *See* Id. (factors like nature and extent of contamination at the site, dollar amount for cleanup, degree of consideration for insurance, successor liability, and contribution issues)
[152] *See* Id. at 350.
[153] *See* Id.
[154] *See* Id.
[155] *See* Id.

judicially determined – fearing that such evidence could constitute admissions in a subsequent cost recovery cleanup action[156].

The Supreme Court in Atlantic Research[157], court revived PRP's direct claims against other responsible parties under § 107(a) of CERCLA and rejected the law in almost every circuit that PRP claims were limited to those in contribution under § 113 of CERCLA[158]. Now, PRP's can now assert 107(a) direct claims against another PRP and thereby potentially escape the consequences of section 502(e)(1)(B)'s bar against certain contribution claims[159]. There, PRP's can obtain indirect relief by filing their own proof of claim[160].

I. Priority Administrative Claims, Response Costs necessary to Provide for Estate[161]

Monetary claims for cleanup costs incurred prepetition, if allowed, are general unsecured, dischargeable claims, the holders of which are entitled to distributions on a pro rata basis with other general unsecured creditors after satisfaction of all secured and priority claims[162]. Similarly, future response costa arising from pre-bankruptcy release of contaminants, if allowed, are also general unsecured dischargeable claims[163]. However, priority administrative expense status is generally for actually incurred postpetition to remedy contamination at the debtor's site that poses an imminent danger to the public health and environment[164].

---

[156] See Id. (a claim may be so small as not to warrant the litigation costs or risks inherent in pursing the claim).
[157] United States v. Atlantic Research Corp., 551 US 128 (2007).
[158] See Id. FN supra at 156.
[159]
[160] (failure could lead to a surrogate proof claim by the government, that is, where they may elect to take over prosecution of the claim (or) PRP may vote in name of Government for leverage)
[161] See Id. 351.
[162] See Id.
[163] See Id.
[164] See Id.

Or, that brings the debtor's operations into compliance with applicable environmental laws, otherwise benefits the estate, or improves the value of the debtor's property when the remediation is necessary to preserve the Bankruptcy estate and confers an actual postpetition benefit upon it, where the claims only obtain administrative expense status if they arise from a transaction with the debtor in possession or trustee and it benefits or preserves the estate postpeition[165].

J. Prepetition Settlement Agreements as Executory Contracts, Effect on the Estate[166]

Chapter 11 allows debtors the ability to reject or assume executory contracts and unexpired leases, subject to court approval[167]. The purpose is to convent burdensome obligations of the debtor into a damages claim against the debtor in favor of the aggrieved party[168].

To effectuate an assumption, the debtor must cure all presumption defaults, and the expense of doing so is given priority administrative status[169]. If there are material unperformed obligations on the part of both parties such that the failure of either party to perform would constitute a material breach of the contract excusing performance of the other (or) Judgment or judicial orders* (or) settlement agreement containing consensual obligations merely approved by a court[170]. This may constitute contracts and, if executory at the time of the debtor's bankruptcy, may never be capable of rejection or assumption[171].

---

[165] *See* Id.
[166] *See* Id. at 351
[167] *See* Id.
[168] *See* Id.
[169] *See* Id.
[170] *See* Id.
[171] *See* Id.

a. Successor Liability Issues Peculiar to Bankruptcy, Awareness[172]

Successor liability applies in CERCLA cases and has been applied to CERCLA cases involving asset purchaser in several circuits[173]. The courts, broadening the scope substantially, have held that the asset purchaser does not acquire the seller's liabilities[174]. However, this question turns to the extent to which the purchaser knew or should have known (or inquired) about the potential CERCLA liabilities[175]. For instance, real estate purchaser potentially liable under CERCLA by virtue of its present or former ownership of the contaminated real estate, regardless of asset successorship issues[176].

Does exposure exist based on the bankruptcy seller's presale conduct at or in relationship to a site that the debtor neither owned or operated or sold to the purchaser? Such a claim is necessarily bared as against the asset purchaser, regardless of section 363(f) in the BC; however, because it did not "arise" until after the bankruptcy proceeding was concluded, then a section 363(f) sale free and clear "does not bar such claim" for CERCLA[177]. Without a uniform rule, any asset purchase whose sale is approved by the bankruptcy risks exposure to successor liability, that is, be aware of its potential exposure for the bankrupt seller's yet undisclosed CERCLA liability[178].

---

[172] *See* Id. at 352.
[173] *See* Id.
[174] *See* Id.
[175] *See* Id.
[176] *See* Id.
[177] *See* Id.
[178] *See* Id.

b. Protections for Lenders and Fiduciaries, Control Equals less Risk[179]

In 1996 Congress enacted the Asset Conservation, Lender liability, and Deposit Insurance Protection Act (Asset conversation Act)[180]. This amended CERCLA's liability provisions response to the imposition of CERCLA liability upon lenders and fiduciaries[181].

There, 11th circuit *Fleet Factors* were highlighted: lender merely having the capacity to influence or the right to control the debtor's disposal practices or contaminated property could be held liable as owner or operator under CERCLA, regardless of the degree of actual control it exercised reducing risk[182]. Now, fiduciary is broadly defined to include persons acting as trustee, but liability is typically limited to the assets of the person or entity for whom the trustee is acting[183].

c. Insurance for Environmental Claims, The Details[184]

The existence of coverage for an environmental claim may justify modification of the stay so as to permit the creditor to establish the nature and extent of the debtor's liability, particularly if costs of defense are a covered item[185]. The coverage can increase the value of the estate, either by offsetting corresponding environmental obligations or by providing an alternative source of payment on account of real property secured claims[186].

Therefore, lenders should be careful to promptly perfect security interests not only in the applicable insurance policies but also in policy proceeds an in the debtor's right to sue the

---

[179] *See* Id. at 357.
[180] *See* Id. at 354.
[181] *See* Id.
[182] *See* Id.
[183] *See* Id. (liability only to be satisfied out of the assets of the bankruptcy case)
[184] *See* Id.
[185] *See* Id.
[186] *See* Id.

insurer, paying close attention to such details may ultimately result in the lender's exclusive access to policy proceeds, rather than the proceeds being available to satisfy all claims[187].

Because insurance policies are property of the bankruptcy estate, proceeds of a policy are estate property depends upon the insurance contract and the particular facts of the case[188]. Absence of a mass tort, however, the proceeds are generally do not belong to an estate[189]. And, counsel is advised to consult with bankruptcy and insurance specialists to determine if a policy provides coverage for a specific environmental liability of the debtor, triggered, and determining parties with interests in the policy[190].

IV. CONCLUSION

In conclusion, whether the EPA, SEC, or DOJ comes knocking on your door, (or) whether you are on the other side of the regulator's table; (or) whether you are turning corners for the Government; everyone is left to the will of a Bear-of-a-statute ("CERCLA") in the Woods with a framework and 'fresh-start' ("Bankruptcy Code").

Whether the environment- contaminated, abandoned, and so forth- is treated as a claim is a question where tensions exist between CERCLA & the Bankruptcy Code (and) where the Devil is in the Details.

---

[187] *See* Id.
[188] *See* Id.
[189] *See* Id.
[190] *See* Id.

www.ingramcontent.com/pod-product-compliance
Lightning Source LLC
Chambersburg PA
CBHW031942170526
45157CB00008B/3282